HANDS-ON ALASKA

ART ACTIVITIES FOR ALL AGES

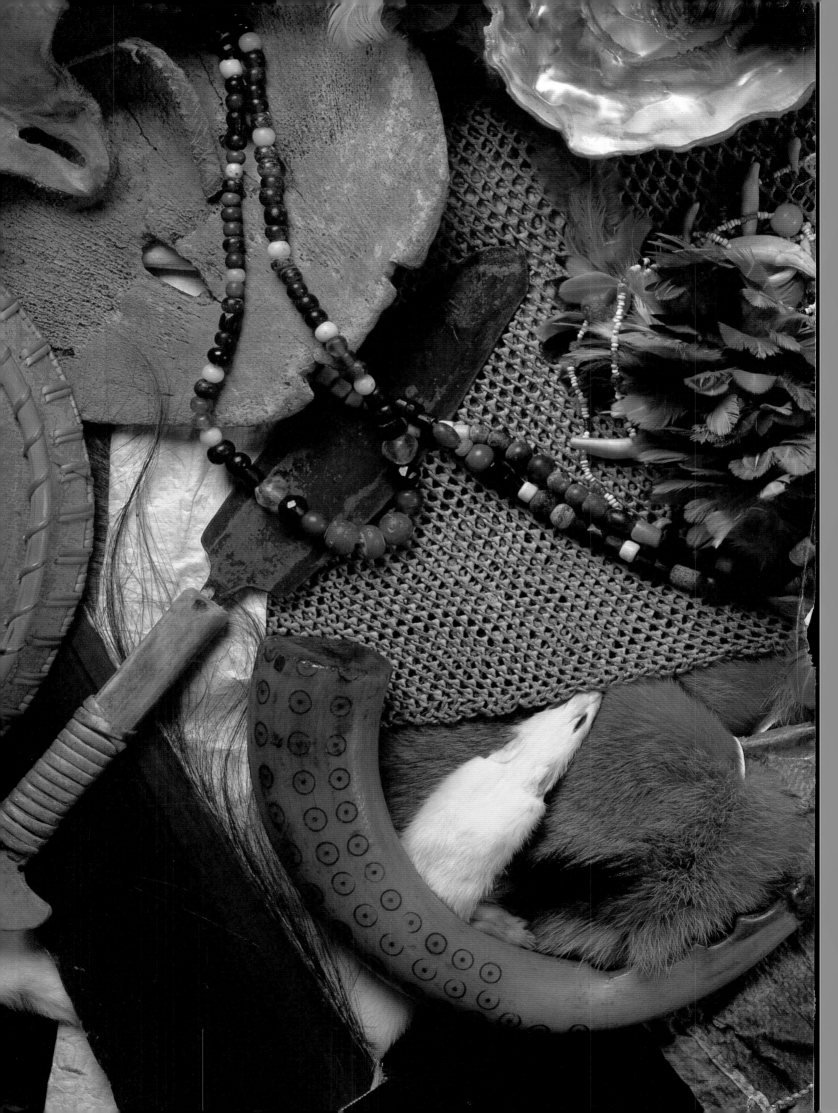

This book is dedicated to Melinda, Tessa and Emily who
grew up in Alaska crafting at the
kitchen table in Stuckagain Heights.

Book design and photography
Art & International Production,
Anchorage, Alaska
Jim Tilly and Sasha Sagan
Special thanks to Sergei Didyk and
Jennifer Moody for technical support.

Alaska Native information
edited by Susan W. Fair
Text edited by Molly Jones
Art Projects drawn and tested by
Jody Jenkins and Mary Simpson
with students and friends.

Other books by the author
from KITS Publishing:

Hands-on Africa
(ISBN 0-9643177-7-X)

Hands-on Alaska
(ISBN 0-9643177-3-7)

Hands-on Asia
(ISBN 0-9643177-5-3)

Hands-on Celebrations
(ISBN 0-9643177-4-5)

Hands-on Rocky Mountains
(ISBN 0-9643177-2-9)

Hands-on Latin America
(ISBN 0-9643177-1-0)

Hands-on Pioneers*
(ISBN 1-57345-085-5)

KITS PUBLISHING
2359 E. Bryan Avenue   Salt Lake City, Utah 84108
(801) 582-2517   fax: (801) 582-2540
e-mail - info@hands-on.com   web - www.hands-on.com
*Published by Deseret Book

First printing, September, 1994, Second printing, April 2000
Printed in Hong Kong

Library of Congress Catalog Card Number: 94-78752
ISBN 0-9643177-3-7

HANDS-ON ALASKA

ART ACTIVITIES FOR ALL AGES

YVONNE Y. MERRILL

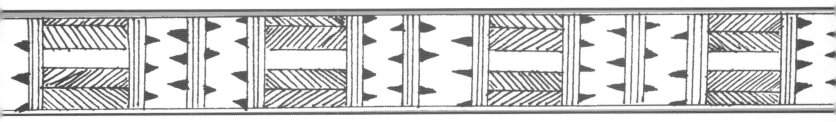

KITS PUBLISHING

TRADITIONAL ALASKA NATIVE ART

Art was an integral part of everyday life for Alaska Native peoples for thousands of years and it remains so for Native artists working in both rural and urban areas today. In times past, there was no specific classification for "artist" within most groups, although artistic expression and shamanism were often combined.

The tradition of excellence of Alaska Native art is inspiring and especially remarkable given the few raw materials available. Before contact with European explorers and traders, all simple tools, containers, clothes, shelters, boats, sleds and ceremonial objects were made from the natural world. Trade often took place over very long distances, and materials like reindeer skins, glass beads, copper, and dentalium shells were widely desired for use in art production. After European contact, new materials became available, and today Native artists use whatever is available to make their art and convey their message—materials like alabaster and plastic—whether they are "traditional" or not.

In the past, materials used by men were usually hard. Wood, for example, was widely used by all groups for ceremonial objects, tools, and containers; stone, bone, and antler were also important. Walrus ivory was prized. Woman's arts tended to be made from softer materials: skins, grasses, feathers, birch bark, and intestine. Skin sewing and skin-processing were among the most important ways a woman could demonstrate her talents. Quills, bird beaks, hair and whiskers were used as trim to finish products.

Most traditional objects made by Native peoples were carefully crafted and designed to celebrate the animals which might be taken with such tools. Many individual pieces rank with the finest art from any culture in the world, even though most were meant to be useful. But most of these works were not designed to last. A totem pole might decay quietly in the forest and a clan house could fall to ruins as people moved to a new location, a group of masks burned after a ceremony was completed.

Alaska Native art is thriving today, and some older forms considered lost are being revitalized, such as the Chilkat blanket of the Northwest Coast Indians and Aleut bentwood hats. Most Native artists feel an obligation to pass their skills on to younger artists. Non-Natives also celebrate the brilliant story of Alaska's Native cultures by creating works influenced by traditional objects.

Beaufort Sea

Barrow

Brooks Range

Koyukuk River

Yukon River

Fairbanks

Tanana Riv

Mt. McKinley

ATHABASKAN

Palmer

Glenallen

Anchorage

Seward

Lake Iliamna

Homer

Yakutat

Haines

Juneau

Gulf of Alaska

Kodiak Is.

Sitka

Ketchikan

NORTHWEST COAST

NORTHWEST COAST INDIANS

Along the rugged coast of the North Pacific Ocean from Cape Mendocino, California, to Alaska's Yakutat Bay, live a number of Indian tribes who share cultural similarities and are known collectively as Northwest Coast peoples. Here, the warm Japanese current flows along the coast, preventing extremely cold temperatures. The weather is moderate, rainy, and stable. Bounded by the mountains from the interior, the region nourishes North America's only rain forest and supports abundant sea-life including marine mammals, fish, and waterfowl. The rich salmon runs of a few weeks' duration provide most villages with enough food for most of the year, though processing the large quantity of fish is time-consuming and laborious.

TOTEM POLES

TOTEM POLES

Materials: construction paper (12" x 18"), cardboard paper tube, light colored chalk, markers, oil crayons, scissors, masking tape, glue.

1.   Study Northwest Coast totem figures.

2.   Choose one figure that you would like to create. Experiment with this figure before you add more.

3.   With chalk, lightly draw your interpretation of the traditional figure on the construction paper. (Use the paper the tall way.) Use the whole sheet of paper.

4.   Color in with oil crayons. Remember to use only the traditional colors on the figure itself (red, blue-green, white and black). You may use other colors to fill in the space around your figure.

5.   Make several more totem figures for your story.

6.   You may glue and tape them to your paper tubes.

IDEA:
    Think about an animal that interests you. Can you do a legend or totem pole that tells about it?

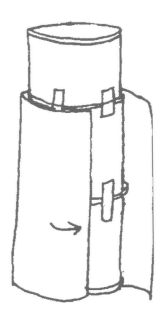

BASIC DESIGN FORMS

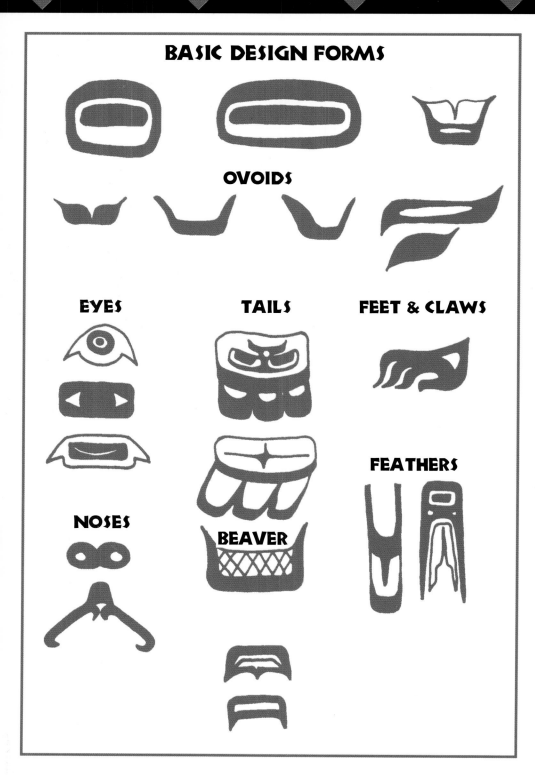

OVOIDS

EYES

TAILS

FEET & CLAWS

FEATHERS

NOSES

BEAVER

The totem pole has become the best-known single image of the Northwest Coast Indians. The impressive height represents concern with ancestry and status, as well as the fact that the rain forest contributes grand, worthy trees. Poles called house-posts were also used inside the corners of clan houses. The images of animals, birds, and legendary creatures carved into the poles are clan symbols or crests. A totem pole was carved as a memorial to an important person, to record an important event, to depict a story, or sometimes to embarrass someone. They were symbols of wealth and family pride. A potlatch was usually held when a new totem pole was installed.

Donna Matthews designed the presentation of the design forms.

CEREMONIAL RATTLE

CEREMONIAL RATTLE

Materials: paper bowls (two per person), several rolls of masking tape, cardboard scraps, scissors, glue, construction paper scraps (red, black, and blue-green), brown shoe polish (either liquid or paste), wooden stick or old pencil (one per person), black markers, beans.

1.   Cut shapes out of cardboard scraps for the facial features of your rattle such as the beak.

2.   Tape the features onto one of the paper bowls. Next cover each feature and the bowl completely with the masking tape. It works best when you tear the tape into small pieces about 1" to 2" long.

3.   Tape both bowls together as shown. Continue taping until the bowls and the shapes are completely covered.

4.   Gently push 10-12 beans into 1" space at bottom.

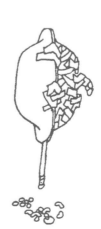

5.   Insert a wood stick or a pencil between the bowls at the center bottom. Tape it into place.

6. Paint or rub the tape with shoe polish. Liquid brown polish can be applied directly, but paste polish must be rubbed on with a soft, clean rag. Let dry.

7. For the mouth, and eyes, cut shapes out of construction paper. Use only black, red, and blue-green paper. Glue into place. (Paint may be used in place of paper shapes.) Use real feathers if you wish.

8. Use markers for details.

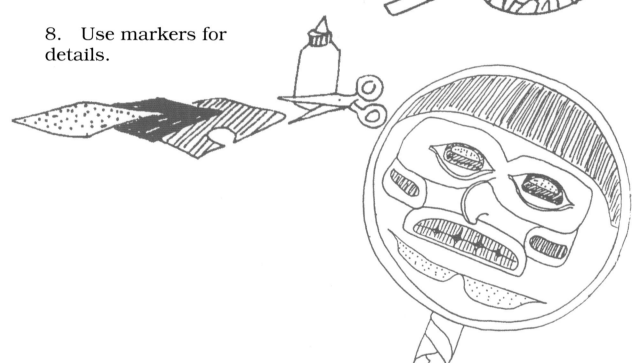

Medicine men, called shamans, were believed to have supernatural powers including the ability to communicate with other realms. A shaman could control the weather, predict the future, bring success in warfare or hunting, cure disease, and find those who were lost.

The shaman often produced his art himself. The shaman's rattle was a prized and sacred object commonly made in the form of a hawk. Similar rattles portrayed ravens, thunderbirds, or eagles. They were used to assist the healer in calling upon helpful spirits. Various teeth, shells, and bird beaks sewn into the fringes of sha-mans' clothing also made rustling and rattling sounds as they moved, adding to the drama of their presence.

CEREMONIAL HAT

CEREMONIAL HAT

Materials: cardboard (18" x 18"), glue, scissors, markers or water colors, tempera paint, paper cups, thread, strings and found objects such as feathers, beads and buttons.

1. The ceremonial hat of the Northwest Coast Indian often represents a certain clan symbol such as a whale, eagle, or raven. Look at the designs on Northwest Coast Indian art forms to get ideas for decorating your hat. Use construction paper, markers, or paint. Try to use only white, red, blue-green, or black colors.

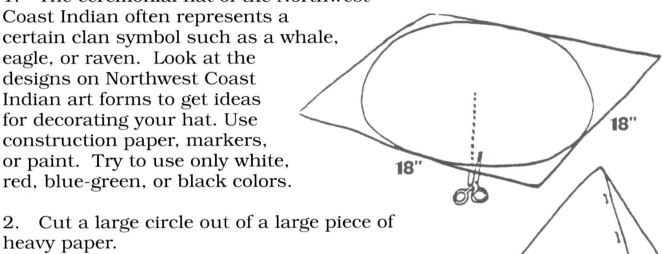

2. Cut a large circle out of a large piece of heavy paper.

3. Cut a slit from one edge to the center of the circle. Slide one flap of this slit over the other to create a cone shape to fit your head. Staple or glue in place.

4. Create your own symbol for the top of your hat. Begin with a short cylinder made of paper glued to the top.

Northwest Coast hats were carved from wood or woven out of cedar bark and painted with crest signs. This style of hat was commonly worn by a person of high status and was often surmounted by a number of woven cylinders called "potlatch rings." Each ring represented a potlatch he had hosted.

FIGURE RATTLE

FIGURE RATTLE

Materials: cardboard scraps, toilet paper tubes, scissors, glue, black, red, and blue-green markers, hole punch, dried beans.

1. Look at the various figure rattles made by the Northwest Coast Indians.

2. Use a cardboard tube as the base of your rattle. Enclose the ends by tracing each end onto cardboard and gluing one round shape into place.

3. Insert dried beans into rattle.

4. Punch a hole with a sharp object and insert a pencil into the hole for a handle. Glue the pencil in place, and then glue the round shape onto the end of the tube.

5. Decorate with shapes cut out of cardboard. Glue and let dry.

6. Color with markers, using only the traditional colors of red, black, and blue-green. If possible, draw first with a small, fine-tip black marker, then color in.

Note: You may use any heavy paper container in place of the paper tube. Make certain that it does not have a waxy surface.

A raven riding atop the back of a curved bird head was a common theme for the rattle carving of a shaman, chief, or headman. The raven was a culture hero, responsible for the creation of mankind. It was the raven who had pried open a clam shell, bringing light to the world through a clever trick and creating the animals that inhabit the earth. Raven rattles were occasionally used in warfare as well as in healing ceremonies and clan celebrations.

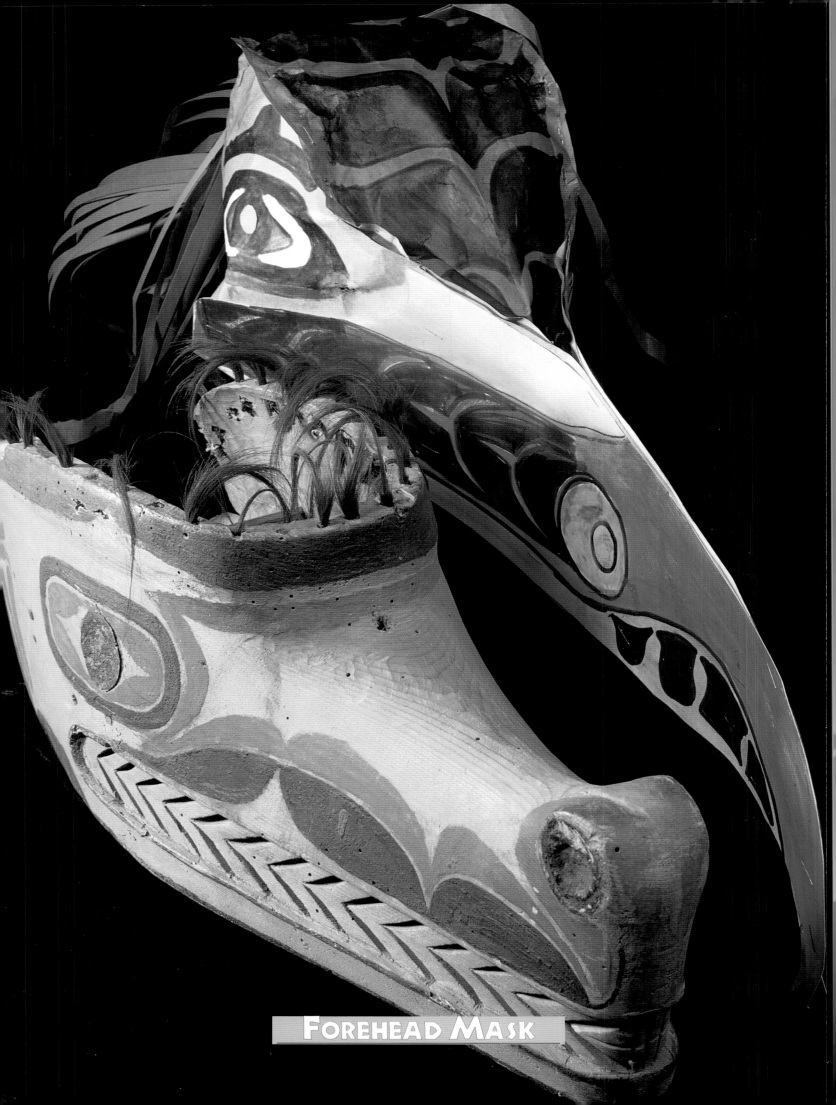

FOREHEAD MASK

FOREHEAD MASK

Materials: thin cardboard or poster board (about 6"x 30") scraps of the same kind of paper (either cardboard or poster board), glue, scissors, assortment of construction paper scraps (black, white, red, and blue-green only), stapler, found objects.

1. Study the designs of Northwest Coast Indian art. Look at different forehead masks.

2. With the help of a friend take the 6"x 30" piece of cardboard and staple it together around your head as shown.

3. Glue the two ends together.

4. Choose the animal your mask will depict (wolf, raven, eagle, etc.).

5. Cut out the shape of your animal.

6. With scraps of the same kind of cardboard you are using, construct features of your mask such as ears, eyes, nose, tongue, and teeth. Glue in place or use a stapler for larger shapes.

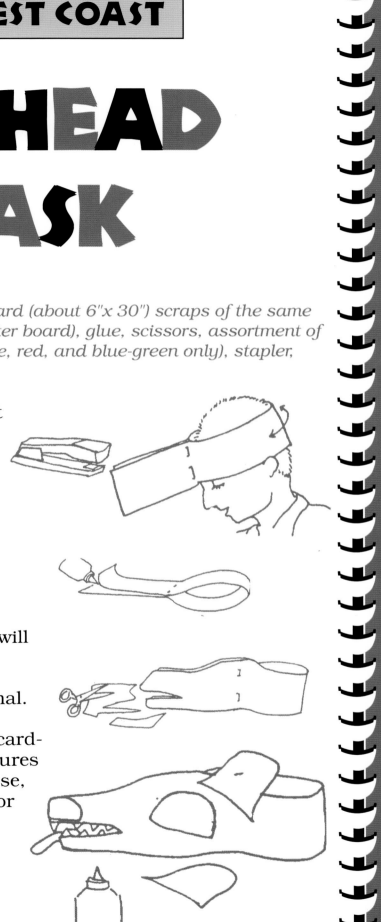

7.   Use construction paper to decorate your mask with the elements of Northwest Coast Indian design. Cut out shapes from black, red, or blue-green paper or add color to the shapes. Glue onto your mask.

8.   Use masking tape or a stapler to join heavy materials such as paper, fake grass or leather.

NOTE:
Any size cardboard strip can be used for the basic form of this mask.

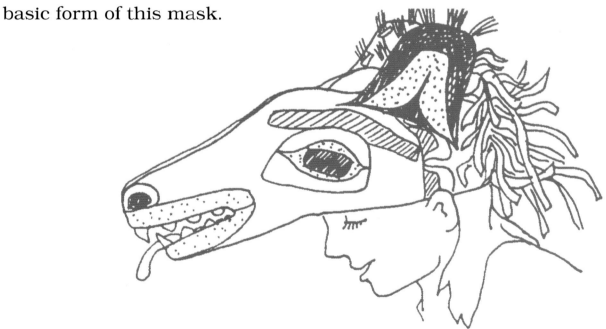

Ceremonial dances among some groups, especially the Kwaikiutl of British Columbia, sometimes features dancers wearing feather costumes and enormous bird-beak masks. Usually the lower jaw opened and clacked shut with the dancer's movement by means of hidden strings and other devices, creating a dramatic effect in the dim firelight of the clan house.

OCTOPUS BAG

OCTOPUS BAG

Materials: dark colored paper (two 12" x 18" sheets), oil crayons, scissors, glue, hole punch, string, colored paper scraps.

1. Look at traditional octopus bags.

2. Choose a shape that you like. Below are three traditional designs. Draw one of them as large as you can on one of your 12"x 18" sheets of paper.

3. Cut it out.

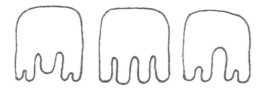

4. Place a thin line of glue along all of the edges of the bag except the top.

5. Glue this first shape to the other piece of 12" x 18" paper.

6. Cut out your octopus bag.

7. Study the stylized floral designs used by the Tlingit and Athabaskan Indians.

8. With oil crayons, draw and color in the floral shapes on the dark paper or cut out designs and glue.

9. Make a long handle with string. Tape or staple it onto the inside of your bag.

10. Use a hole punch on brightly colored scraps of paper. Glue the circles to your bag. You can also glue objects onto your bag to represent beads or buttons.

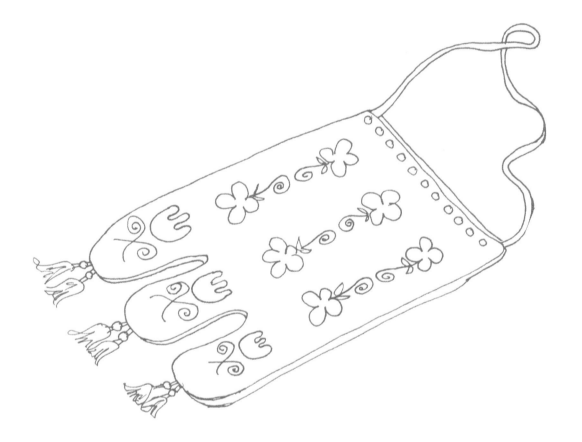

Octopus bags, named because of their unusual shape, became highly prized among both Northwest Coast and Athabaskan peoples. After contact with European traders, floral designs were often chosen for the beadwork on the bags, which were made of wool-trade cloth. It is difficult to tell Athabaskan-made octopus bags from those made by the Tlingit, but it is thought that the interior Athabaskans traded many of these bags for prized dentalium shells.

PUPPET PERSON & CHILKAT TUNIC

Puppet Person & Chilkat Tunic

Materials: cardboard scraps (8" x 4"), scissors, glue, hole punch, brass brads, flat stick, masking tape, crayons, found objects (fabric, fur, feathers, leather, etc.), string.

1. On your piece of cardboard draw the head and body of your puppet. Cut it out.

2. On the second piece of cardboard draw the legs and arms. Cut them out.

3. Punch a hole at the top of both shoulders and on the top of both arm shapes. Attach with a brad.

4. Do the same with the legs.

5. When the legs and arms are assembled, attach the stick on the back with tape and glue.

6. Cut four strings. Punch a small hole at the top of both arms and legs with a pencil or hole punch. Tie string to each hole as shown. Tie the ends of the four strings together.

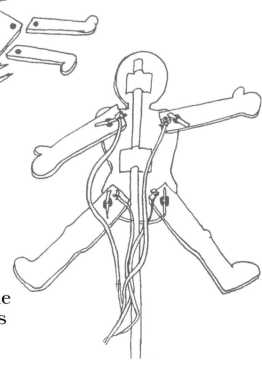

7. Pull on the strings to make arms and legs move. Loosen the brads if movement is stiff.

8. Measure your Chilkat tunic with your puppet figure.

9. Design your crest symbol and fill in the spaces.

10. Use black, red, blue-green and yellow markers.

11. Dress your Northwest Coast Indian figure in grass woven boots, a chief hat and a Chilkat tunic.

Twined Chilkat weavings were objects of great value. Robes, aprons, and tunics were woven of mountain goat wool and shredded bark. Such important ceremonial garments were usually danced, or worn, at a potlatch. Often, a deceased elder or an important person was wrapped in such a garment during the time of viewing and burial.

A single blanket might take up to six months for one woman to weave. It was traditional for a man to design the pattern, paint half of it on a "pattern board" and for a woman to weave the piece completing the symmetrical design. Most robes were blue-green, yellow, and black on a white background. Blue-green was derived from copper, black from salmon eggs and graphite, and white from the powder of ground clam shells and the natural wool itself. Occasionally, red dye, made from iron oxide and the inner bark of the hemlock tree, was used.

PORTRAIT MASK

PORTRAIT MASK

Materials: paper plates, large 1" or 3/4" brushes, white glue containers (such as school lunch milk cartons), paper scraps in red, black, and blue-green (butcher paper or construction paper), a neutral colored paper (such as brown wrapping paper), paper bag or tissue paper, scissors, hole punch, string.

1. Study Northwest Coast Indian portrait masks.

2. Cut facial features out of paper plate, such as eyes and mouth.

3. Glue on other features, such as ears or nose with scrap white poster board.

4. Mix glue with water in container, one part water to two parts glue.

5. Tear brown paper or neutral colored butcher paper (paper bag, wrapping paper or tissue) into small pieces. Torn strips of masking tape will also work.

6.   Apply liquid glue to mask with brush. Cover mask with pieces of masking tape or small pieces of torn paper, making certain there is glue under and on top of each piece. Overlap the pieces to cover the paper plate completely.

7.   You may let dry or continue by cutting Northwest Coast designs out of red, black, or blue-green paper. Glue these onto your mask.

8.   Give one last "coat" of liquid glue to your mask to seal all shapes and to give it a glossy finish.

9.   Punch holes in the sides and tie string for wearing.

10. Trim the edges of your mask with scissors.

The mask-maker's task was to create an object that would provide a memorable impression in a theatrical setting. Face masks were made for such purposes as the performance of dances re-enacting legends and for shaman's healing ceremonies. Portrait masks may have been made to honor particular people. Masks were worn by both men and women, although they were mainly carved by men. Facial painting and tattoo marks were applied to the carved masks.

ALEUT

The ancestral home of the Aleuts (a lee oot), the Unangan (oo nan guhn) and the Unangas (oo nan guhs), is a thousand-mile long chain of islands that arcs into the Bering Sea. On these treeless windy islands, the Aleuts learned over thousands of years to harvest an extraordinarily rich coastal and marine environment which teemed with whales, otters, and sea lions as well as birds and edible seaweed of various types. Aleut kayak hunters became consummate masters of the sea, while the Aleut women developed

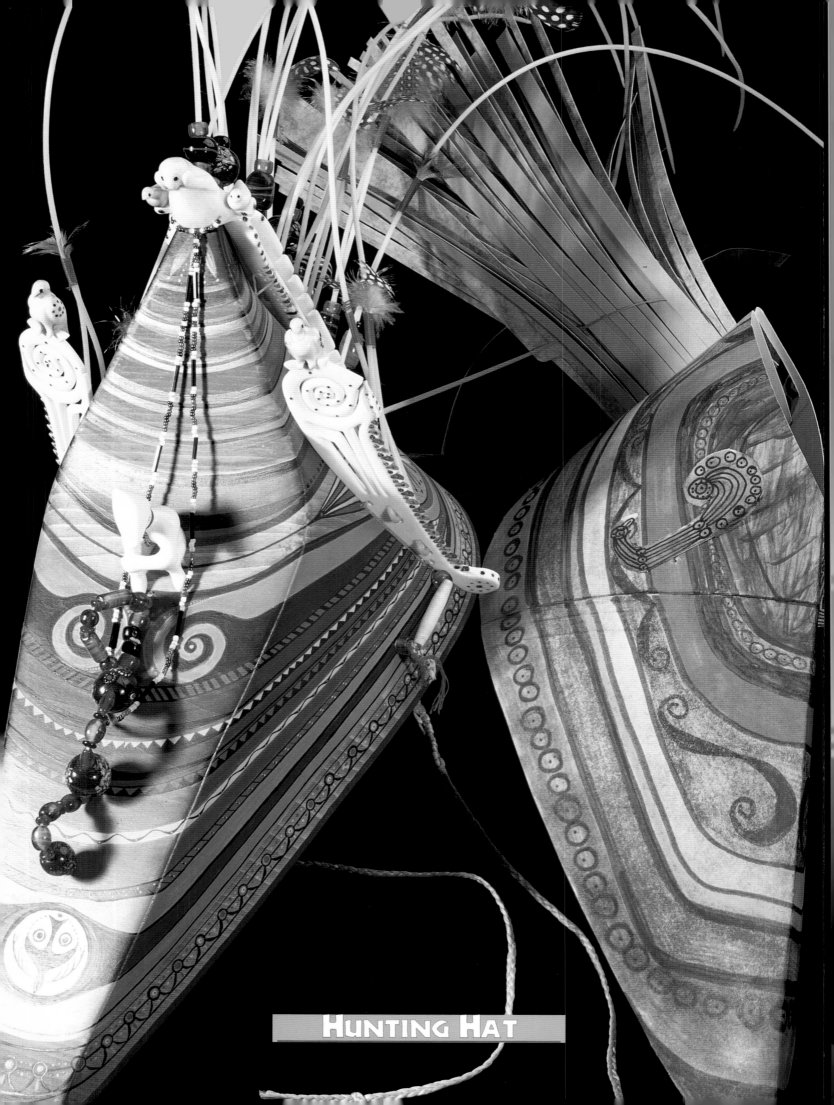

HUNTING HAT

HUNTING HAT

Materials: heavy paper or tagboard, markers, string, and found objects (grasses, reed, buttons, beads, etc.).

1. First cut a long pointed oval or egg shape out of a 12" x 18" sheet of paper.

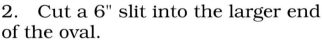
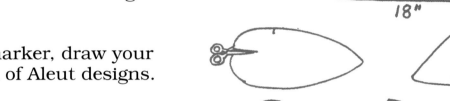

2. Cut a 6" slit into the larger end of the oval.

3. Using a marker, draw your interpretation of Aleut designs.

4. Slide one side of the cut slit over the other side and staple into place.

5. Add details with found objects.

You can also attach an inset to the hat back:

6. Cut a triangle piece of cardboard. Measure the hat's back edge. (A)

7. Score folds one inch toward the center on each side with a scissors point and a straight edge. (B) This is how your triangle looks. (C)

8. Lay the triangle flat on a pile of newspapers. With a big nail, hammer 4 or 5 holes into the center spine of the triangle. (D) You are going to cut 12-15 inch 1/4" cardboard strips. These are going to be the whiskers that will be pushed into the holes after you have attached the back triangle.

9. Next sew or staple the hat edges over the triangle piece. (E)

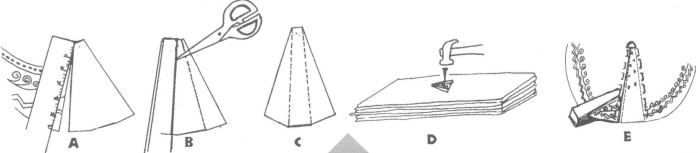

A   B   C   D   E

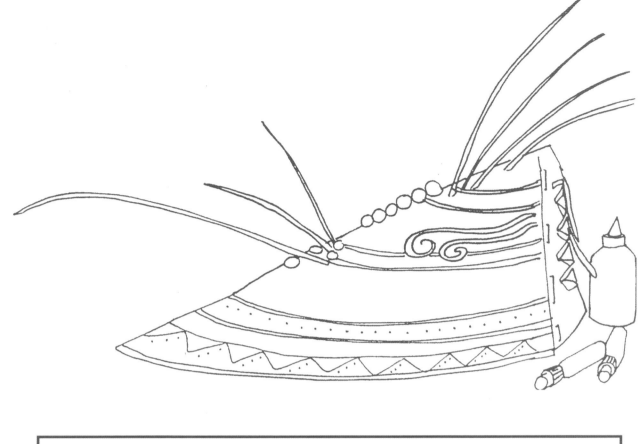

ALEUT ART IDEAS

A story is told that when the Russians peered down from their ships to see the Aleuts in their *bidarkas,* they could not identify the chief. They asked that the head man wear a distinguishing hat with designs that could be seen from above. Perhaps what they wanted, instead, was identification of the most skillful hunters and men of the highest rank.

Bentwood hats were steamed, bent, hollowed, and shaped in several forms. These include open and closed-crowned hats, and hats with visors both long and short. The colorful painted patterns on the hats are reminiscent of Russian folk art, while the ivory carvings atop the hats and the wing-shaped side pieces are probably good luck charms. Animals like sea otters were known to be drawn to beautiful objects such as brightly ornamented hats and elaborate garments.

Gut Parka

GUT PARKA

Materials: white or light tan tissue paper (one sheet 9" x 12") or clothing for a jointed figure, scissors, glue, fine tip markers (red, black, brown, blue), construction paper.

1. Look at the designs and construction of the gut parkas and clothing made by the Aleuts.

2. Cut tissue paper into thin strips (about 1" wide).

3. Glue all the strips together by overlapping as shown.

4. Choose the parka design you wish to create and cut it out of tissue paper. You may choose a traditional parka shape or a new invention of your own.

5. Choose a large sheet of construction paper. Cut and glue a picture of a grassy island environment onto the construction paper.

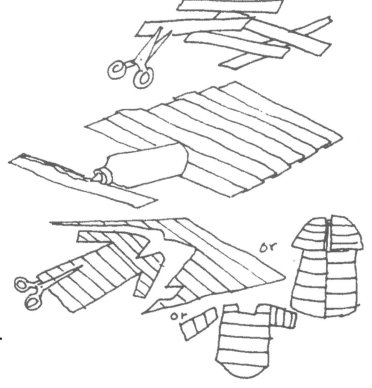

6.   Glue your gut parka figure onto the environment or dress a puppet. (See page 24 for instructions.)

7.   Complete the person wearing the parka with markers, cut paper, or crayons. Add any details.

8.   You may also use found objects such as real grass, pebbles, moss, etc. for your background.

9.   Complete the parka with designs, yarn, feather tufts and decorative stitches by using fine-tip markers.

Another type of parka, made of sea mammal intestine, was lightweight and waterproof. These garments were used particularly by kayak hunters but were also preferred by shamans, who considered the translucent material a path to other worlds. Still other overgarments, especially among the Alutiiq, were made from glossy birdskins, often of contrasting colors and patterns.

ARMOR

ALEUT

ARMOR

Materials: cardboard, masking or strapping tape, scissors, markers.

1.   Cut the cardboard into 1" or 1/2" strips. It is easiest to cut on a paper cutter. All strips should be nearly equal in length.

2.   Lay all the strips about 1/4" apart, as shown.

3.   Tape all the strips together on the top and bottom. Turn the cardboard over and tape the other side, too.

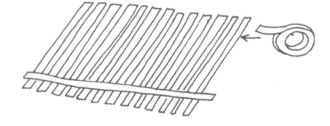

4.   Fold the armor like a vest. Cut the bottom edge straight or curved.

5.   Cut out two arm holes, one on each fold. Leave at least 1" of cardboard above each arm hole.

6.   Tape under each arm hole all the way across armor (and on both front and back).

7.   Trim top edge of vest.

8.   Decorate with markers (black, brown, red, blue). Try to re-create designs that you have seen on various artifacts such as Aleut baskets.

TOP EDGE OF VEST

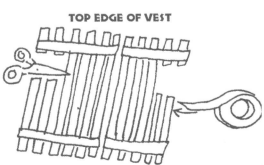

Traditional Aleuts, like other Alaska Native people, had reason to protect themselves from invasion by other groups. Their armor, constructed from slats made of bone, wood or ivory, was laced together and etched with designs.

ESKIMO

The Eskimos of Alaska speak different languages and have cultural differences. The peoples who live along the coast of the Bering Sea in Southwest Alaska are the Yupik (yoo pik). St. Lawrence Island Eskimos inhabit St. Lawrence Island, midway between the continents of North America and Asia. And, in the far north, the Inupiat (in oo pee yat) maintain yet another culture and speak a different language. The Alutiiq (uh loo tik) people live in Prince William Sound and in the Kodiak Island area. They speak a variation of the Eskimo language. Their culture, however, is a combination of Aleut, Eskimo and Northwest Coast.

SPIRIT MASK

ESKIMO
Spirit Mask

Materials: cardboard scraps (a large assortment of sizes and shapes), scissors, glue, tempera paint, liquid dish washing soap, small brushes, milk cartons for paint, newspapers, found objects (feathers, leather, fur scraps, pipe cleaners, etc.), string, hole punch.

1.   Study the designs of various Eskimo spirit masks. Choose a basic form and cut it out of cardboard.

Your mask may be a special animal or spirit, or it may be your own design idea. Use the traditional forms, colors, and textures of the Eskimo people.

2.   Decide if your mask is to be worn or for display only. If it is to be worn, punch three holes as shown for the string. Have a friend help you locate the place for the "eye holes" as you hold your mask in place, mark and cut out. Tie long strings to each hole.

3.   Place the mask on a large piece of dark poster board. Cut a circle which is at least 1 1/2" from the outside of the mask. This strip should be about 1" wide.

4.   Glue the extended parts of your mask to the center face and then to the paper ring. You can also wrap thread around each object to fasten it to the ring. Other hoop materials which are thin, flexible and stiff could be tried.

5.   Mix tempera into small cartons. Add 1/4 cup dish washing liquid to 1 cup paint to help it adhere without chipping. Use a variety of these colors: brown, white, black, red, yellow, blue, green, and orange. Put two brushes in each milk carton (one small fine brush and one medium brush).

6.   Paint the mask. Leave the cardboard plain where the "look" of natural wood is desired.

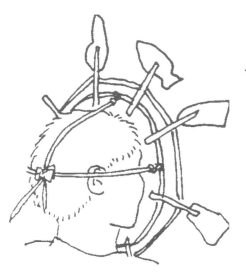

7. Add found objects.

8. Attach the strings together as shown with the help of a friend.

   Masks and puppets made by Eskimo peoples, especially those of the Yupik, exhibit deep, symbolic, and complicated connections with the natural world. They often express emotion as well--a sense of humor or fear--or the power of a spirit-being who controls hunting success. Long ago when a special celebration was held, guests might be greeted by a talking bird puppet, operated by a ventriloquist-shaman, that swooped down from the community house smoke hole and teased them.

   The hooped mask associated with the Yupik represents the cosmos of this group in miniature. This mask was usually the central element in all dance performances. Its series of rings represent the layers of heaven. The appendages which surround it are often separated characteristics of the central animal or figure but may also be symbolic attachments like pierced hands, designed to allow some animals to slip through to insure future abundance of game.

SCRIMSHAW

Materials: a few sharp tools (safety pin, tack, nail, etc), a used bar of soap, newspapers, colored ink, rags or paper toweling, and a small paint brush.

1. Look at examples of Eskimo scrimshaw.

2. Practice a few designs on a sheet of paper. Look at the lines and patterns on Eskimo art for ideas.

3. With a sharp tool, scratch your design into the smooth, flat side of a bar of soap.

4. Gently rub ink into the surface of the soap with a small brush or a rag. Carefully pat off the excess ink. Do not rub. The ink should remain in the depression scratched into the soap.

Alternatives: Try carving the soap into a simple shape before attempting the scrimshaw. Use a flat box or tray to catch the chips you cut off. (See scrimshaw samples in photograph on page 59.)

SUN GOGGLES

Sun Goggles

Materials: cardboard at least 6" x 6", string, ruler, pencil, sharp scissors or utility knife, brown shoe polish or crayon.

1. Cut out your goggle pattern on a folded piece of paper.

2. Trace around the shape on a piece of tag board or cardboard.

3. Decorate the goggles with a fine-tipped marker.

4. Color with crayon or rub on brown shoe polish.

5. Cut out eye slits.

6. Poke hole at each corner and knot 18" of string.

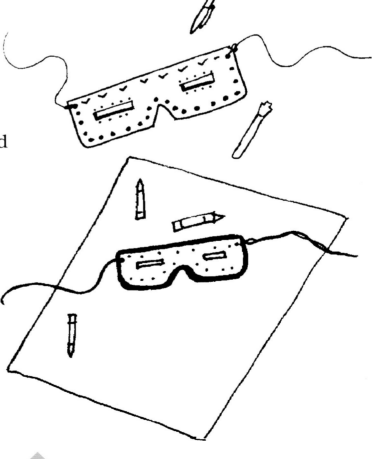

The glare of the arctic sun has always been hard on the eyes. Eskimo sun goggles were important protectors and essential to the hunter's gear. They were carved from ivory, wood or bone. Decorative incising was usually done around the edges and eye holes. The shape varied with the carver.

FINGER MASKS

FINGER MASKS

Materials: small cardboard or posterboard scraps, paper scraps, masking tape, scissors, glue, found objects (fur, feathers, grasses, yarn, etc.), markers or paint, pencils.

1.   Look at traditional Eskimo finger masks.

2.   Choose a basic shape that you like and cut it out of the cardboard. Remember that you need finger holes.

3.   On a scrap of cardboard draw a handle large enough for two "finger holes." It should be at least 2"x 3". (Thick cardboard will be very difficult to cut so you may wish to make two identical handle shapes and glue them together for durability.)

4.   Glue the handle onto the back of your finger mask. Reinforce with a strong heavy strip of cardboard glued over the joint where they meet.

5.   Wrap thin strips of masking tape through and around the finger holes.

6.   Create a 4" trim of cut paper, hair, fur, or grasses. Glue onto the back of the mask or tape into place.

7.   Decorate the front of the finger mask with markers or paint. Can you think of creative ways to use the finger masks?

When Eskimo women dance, their hands are active and expressive while their feet often remain still, and they generally accent their hand movements with finger masks. The central part of the mask, like the face mask, often displays a circle-within-a-circle motif which represents the cosmos. Sometimes finger masks portray a toothy *inua*, or they may represent smiling male guardian spirits, frowning female spirits, or mythical beasts.

COVER-UPS OF FUR OR FEATHERS

COVER-UPS OF FUR OR FEATHERS

Materials: If you want to place your figure in an Arctic environment, you will need a sheet of paper 12" x 18". Or, you may decide to dress a puppet. Other materials are paper scraps, scissors, glue, crayons and found objects for trim such as fur and feathers.

1.   Choose a small sheet of construction paper (at least 4" x 6") similar in color to the type of clothing you wish to make. With a pencil draw the outline of the clothing (parka, pants, or boots.)

2.   Cut out the shapes and color with crayon the texture of fur or feathers. Add scraps of paper or found objects to decorate clothing.

3.   Next create the environment for your person on the large 12" x 18" sheet of construction paper.

    A. First make the sky by cutting a sheet of paper to fit the top of your large paper or by gluing together many small pieces.

    B. Next find and glue paper scraps to fill in the foreground. Where will your person be? On the snow, ice, water, dirt, or grass?

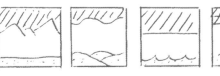

4. Glue the clothing and figure you made onto your environment.

5. Color the person's face, hands, legs, and feet. You may wish to cut out paper scraps to make the details of the person.

6. Add tools, equipment or animals. Use any found objects that you may have.

7. Another option is to dress a puppet. See page 24 for instructions.

Among the Yupik and Inupiat Eskimos as well as some Athabaskan groups, fur parkas of ground squirrel, caribou, and reindeer were the most common winter clothing. Sometimes the fur was turned inside, but when it was out, the parka was decorated with beautifully crafted borders of bleached sealskin embroidered with patterns or, later, complicated geometric pieced calfskin designs. Fancy traditional squirrel skin parkas were adorned with bright tufts of yarn, trade beads, strips of burbot (fish) skin, wolf or wolverine tails, and other materials. These parkas were often worked on by a group of women representing several generations. The materials selected were designed to make the wearer "like" the chosen animal in terms of strength, speed, or intelligence. A combination of wolf and wolverine made the warmest, most attractive ruff.

Women processed all skins, often pegging them out on the tundra to dry or bleach. They cut and constructed all garments, from caps to mukluks and boots, by measuring with their hands, eyes, and bodies, not by using a paper pattern. Most skin sewing was and still is done in the winter, when the light outside is short and women's subsistence activities like berry picking and hanging fish to dry have been long since completed.

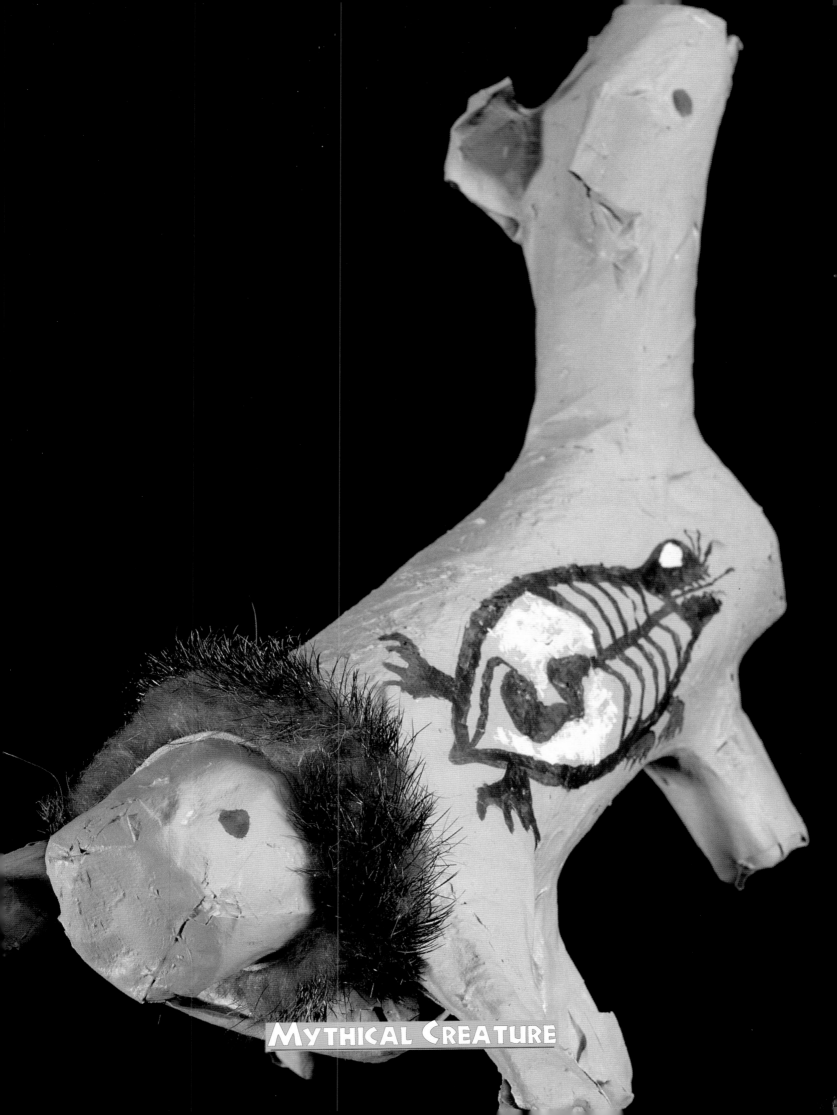

MYTHICAL CREATURE

MYTHICAL CREATURE

Materials: newspaper, flour and water paste, masking tape (several rolls), butcher paper in various colors, paper plates, scissors, cardboard scraps, large plastic dishpan.

1. Create the form for your mythical creature by rolling and wadding newspaper and taping with masking tape. Use a lot of tape. Cut cardboard shapes and tape on for ears, feet, horns, etc.

2. Before pasting, decide on the colors of the creature. Cut or tear the butcher paper into workable sizes.

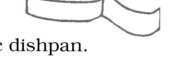

3. Mix flour and water paste in a large plastic dishpan. Start with 1/2 cup of flour and 1/3 cup of water. Mix to a consistency of thick smooth cream.

5. Wipe paste onto a piece of colored butcher paper and smooth onto your creature. Repeat until the form is completely covered. Smooth out uneven edges.

6. Different colors of butcher paper may be added for details while paste is still damp on your form. Wash hands and cut small details from different colors of butcher paper. Smooth onto the wet form.

7. Let dry. No painting is necessary.
You may shellac the finished product if you wish.

IDEA:
This mythical creature provides a
good opportunity for
creative writing.

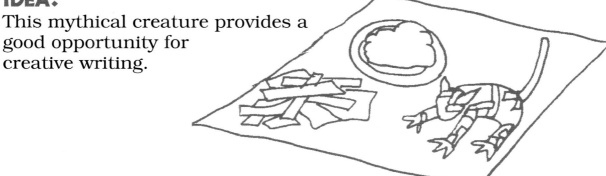

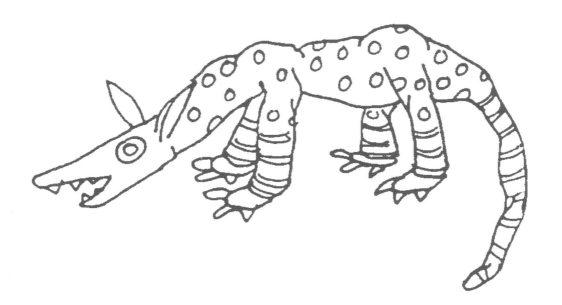

The exploits of heroic figures and tales surrounding imagined creatures
enrich all cultures. Some are secular figures while others have religious connotations. Alaska Natives knew of many fantastic creatures--retold through the
generations in stories and legends--which they depicted in their art. Dragons,
insects, and skeletonized animals were painted, especially on wood, to appease
ominous forces and to bridge the gap between human hunters and their prey.
These artistic works often had religious connotations. One legendary beast
commonly portrayed was the *palraiyuk,* a long, snaky monster with a crocodile-
like head.

ESKIMO
ARCTIC DWELLINGS

Materials: cardboard cut into narrow strips (about 1/4" x 6"), brown paper bags torn into uneven patches of 4" x 4", crayons, scissors, glue, masking tape.

1.   Make the support structure of the dwelling using cardboard strips. They may be joined at the top, tepee style (see A) or laid on top of each other as a foundation for a skin roof (see B).

3 types of skin houses

A.

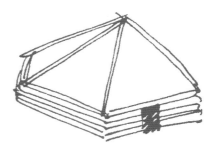

Bowed bone or birch tree trunk with sewn skin covering

Birch trunk tepee

Log with skin roof

B.

2.   To extend the 6" cardboard strips, overlap two lengths and tape at the joint.

Tape on the top.

3.   Cover the cardboard forms with torn, brown paper bag pieces that are shapes of tanned animal skins. Color the paper first with a coating of brown crayon. Use different colors of brown on top of one another, and burnish by rubbing with a tissue or soft cloth. Tape or glue into place.

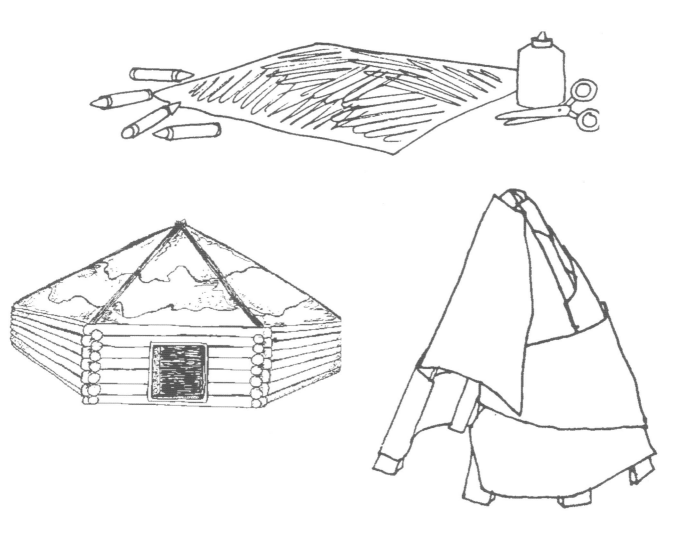

House styles varied with the season, as people often moved from place to place or abandoned a house after a death. The most common type of house throughout the north was a semi-subterranean dwelling, framed of driftwood and covered with a thick layer of sod. Usually a home like this had one gut window in the ceiling and was entered by a long, underground entry way. Light-weight, cone-shaped skin tents were used for summer camping and travel. St. Lawrence Island Eskimos lived in large, domed skin tents with a small interior room called an *agra* in which all family members slept. Alutiiq peoples lived in large, multifamily houses. The snow shelter, or igloo, was almost never con-structed by Alaska Eskimos unless there was an emergency situation.

WILDLIFE CARVINGS

WILDLIFE CARVINGS

Materials: small milk cartons, plaster, sand or vermiculite (optional - makes carving easier) water, sharp tools (knife, nail, file, rasp, etc.), plastic bowl, stirring sticks, newspaper, some coloring materials (shoe polish, wood stains, colored inks, water colors, or oil paints).

1. Work on a sketch of an animal (front, side, top, rear views).

2. Fill one pint milk carton 3/4 full with water. Pour this into a plastic bowl. Add plaster to the water until islands of plaster appear. Add sand (one part sand to one part plaster). Stir swiftly with your hand squeezing the lumps until mixed. (See HINT on page 61.) You can add color such as tempera paint at this step.

3. Mixture thickens quickly, so pour immediately into milk cartons.

4. Let plaster dry. This takes one to two hours, or overnight.

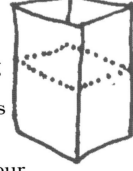

5. Let the remaining plaster in the plastic mixing bowl dry and scrape it out into the waste basket. Do not get plaster into your sink! Use paper towels to wipe off your hands before washing.

6. Peel milk carton from plaster. You can draw your animal sketch directly on the plaster or simply begin carving. Remember to constantly turn the piece as you work on it.

7. As you carve or file away the plaster, work into a shallow cardboard box or nest of newspaper.

8. Use nails, old dental tools, nut picks, etc. for carving lines and descriptive detail.

9. Before coloring the animal you must seal the plaster with white liquid glue (add a little water). Brush on and let dry.

10. Color your dried carving with shoe polish, wood stains, colored inks, water colors, or oil paints. They can be brushed or rubbed onto the carving. Rub off excess with a cloth. Color can be added to wet plaster also.

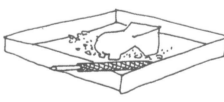

The traditional carving of walrus ivory was confined to the manufacture of hunting tools and personal charms. Many of these objects were richly ornamented, carved and incised with the *inua* of various creatures as well as both decorative and symbolic designs. Many Inupiat artists etched a record of hunts, wars, and other important events into functional pieces like bucket handles and drill bows. At the turn of the century, an Inupiat artist from Nome--Happy Jack--was encouraged to etch ivory for the souvenir trade by Yankee whalers and traders and became the best-known Eskimo artist to do so. Today, the carving and etching of ivory remains an established art.

PICTOGRAPHS

PICTOGRAPHS

Materials: shoe box or other small container, clay, plaster, plastic bucket, stir sticks, sharp-pointed tools, (pencil, nail, pick, etc.), paper clips (one per person), paper, pencil, polymer or white liquid glue, coloring materials (such as shoe polish, wood stains, watercolors, or colored inks.)

1. Study the pictographs of the Eskimo.

2. On a sheet of paper practice creating your own pictograph stories.

3. Emphasize simple, direct figures with little detail. Color in your figure completely with a dark pencil or pen.

4. Prepare your container for plaster casting by putting clay over the entire bottom of the box. Smooth it out evenly. It should be at least 1/2" to 3/4" thick.

(Clay that is mixed with plaster is ruined. Use old clay or modeling clay. Discard clay when finished.)

5. With a sharp tool carve a pictograph design into the clay in the box. Design a border pattern along the sides of the clay. If you make a mistake simply smooth out the clay.

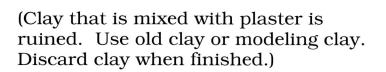

6. Mix a large amount of plaster in a bucket. Pour into the box at least 1" deep.

HINTS:

To mix plaster, pour water into plastic bucket to a half full mark. Next pour in dry plaster until islands appear above water.
Mix with your hand until as smooth and thick as cream, adding more plaster or water as you need it. Work quickly! **Do not wash any plaster down the sink.** Wipe everything off carefully with paper towel before washing.

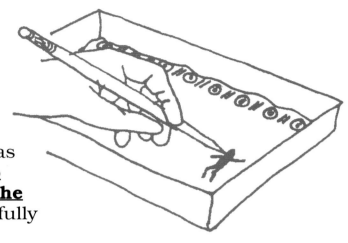

7. Insert a paper clip into the wet plaster in your box for a hook for hanging.

NOTE: THIS PROCESS IS SIMILAR TO THE ACTUAL CARVING TECHNIQUE IN MAKING PICTOGRAPHS; HOWEVER, THE FINAL PRODUCT IS THE REVERSE.

8. Let dry for one to two hours. Remove box and clean off plaster. Coat plaster with polymer medium or white liquid glue and add a little water. Let dry.

Color with shoe polish, wood stains, watercolors, or colored inks. Brush, or rub on and wipe off.

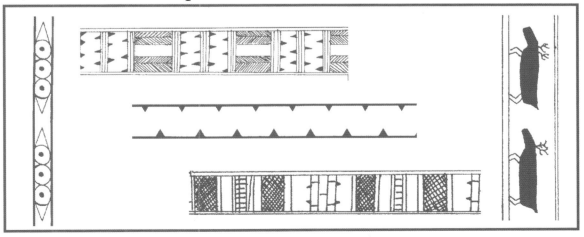

ESKIMO BORDER PATTERNS

ATHABASKAN

The Athabaskan Indians live in the vast interior of Alaska and Canada. These people, all hunters and gatherers, are comprised of eleven separate but closely related groups which speak distinct languages. Few parts of the world demand such difficult survival skills as the Alaskan interior, where temperatures in the short summers reach above 90 degrees Fahrenheit and in the dark, long winter dip as low as -70 degrees.

Birch Bark Basket

BIRCH BARK BASKET

Materials: brown construction paper or paper bag (9"x 12"), scissors, glue, crayons or markers, pencil, hole punch, natural colored string.

1.   Look at the color and texture of birch bark baskets.

2.   Color one side of your sheet of construction paper with many layers of crayon to achieve the look of bark.

3.   Cut your paper from each corner about 3" as shown. Cut straight towards a center point in the middle of the paper.

4.   Fold the two short corners together as shown. Glue, using paper clips to hold together until dry. Fold and glue the two opposite corners.

5.   Cut a triangle shape coming out of both ends.

6.   Fold up the triangles and glue in place.

7.   Decorate the rim of the basket by drawing, gluing on paper or string, or by punching holes along the edge and wrapping yarn through.

You can also make borders with colorful markers and then punch holes along the edge and wrap string or yarn through in an over/under motion.

Both finishes are authentic to Athabaskan baskets.

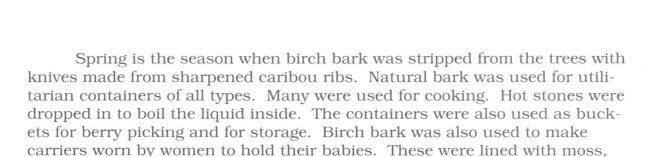

Spring is the season when birch bark was stripped from the trees with knives made from sharpened caribou ribs. Natural bark was used for utilitarian containers of all types. Many were used for cooking. Hot stones were dropped in to boil the liquid inside. The containers were also used as buckets for berry picking and for storage. Birch bark was also used to make carriers worn by women to hold their babies. These were lined with moss, feathers and fur.

Sometimes, dyed willow root trim was used to bind the bark at the top and seams. To make a basket, an Athabaskan woman would soak the bark in water to make it soft and flexible, then fold the corners and sew them tightly with spruce root and, finally, paint pitch along the seams to make them watertight, if necessary.

JEWELRY

ATHABASKAN

JEWELRY

Materials: string, thread, dental floss or fish line, large needles, white drinking straws, potatoes, soaked beans, slices of carrots, broccoli stems and orange peel (all cut up into small pieces), scissors, paper clips.

1. Start with a small handful of straws. Cut them into short sections about 1" long.

2. Thread your needle with a thread about two feet long.

3. Prepare your beads by carefully slicing a handful of carrot and potato pieces, vegetables or orange, lemon or lime peel pieces.

4. Before beginning the necklace, think about various patterns in jewelry.

5. Choose a pattern and begin stringing the straws and vegetables.

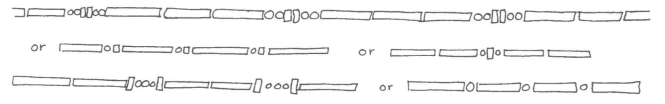

6. When the first thread is completed begin a second strand. Do at least three strands for your necklace. Six strands would best show the pattern for your jewelry. Paper clip the ends together for now.

7. The vegetables should be allowed to dry. Hang your necklace in a warm place. It will take two to three days to dry.

8. When the vegetable parts dry, they may shrink. Slide them close together and tie the strings into a knot.

ATHABASKAN PATTERN IDEAS

White, tubelike shells of dentalium found in the Pacific Ocean were prized by the Athabaskans. All types of goods, including Native copper, were traded for these shells, which were controlled by the coastal Indians. A wealthy Athabaskan family wore dentalium shells on their clothing, pouches, necklaces, headbands, hand and foot gear. These cherished pieces were passed on to other family members, although some exist in museum collections.

THE QUIVER

THE QUIVER

Materials: brown paper bag, crayons or oil pastels, markers, string, scissors, glue and found objects (feathers, beads, etc.), yarn.

1. Study the shape of the Athabaskan quiver. Create your own shape for a quiver and draw it onto the brown paper bag. Cut out two identical quiver shapes.

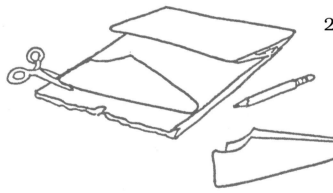

2. Glue the two shapes together along the edges leaving the curved opening unglued.

3. Create your own animal and bird designs with markers to decorate your quiver. One suggestion is to cut out an animal from a piece of paper. Color with markers into the open space left by the animal, using it as a stencil. Repeat this animal shape several times across your quiver.

4. Finish decorating your quiver. Add a handle, feathers, and beads.

Handsome smoke-tanned leathers of caribou and moose made strong sheaths and quivers used to carry knives, lances, and bows and arrows. Most were fringed, beaded and painted with animal figures. They were worn as a daily part of a hunter's clothing. A quiver might be as long as 18". Red ochre, a symbol of creation and abundance, was often rubbed over the skins for color. Feathers, beads, quillwork, embroidery, and charcoal paints were applied.

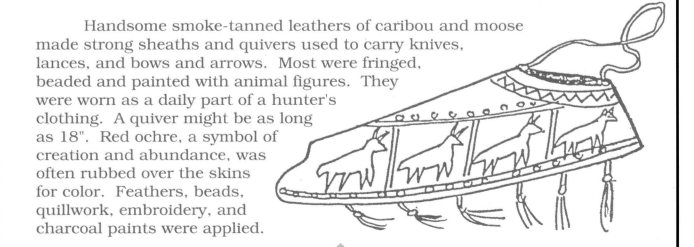

OUTFIT

Outfit

Materials: construction paper (12" x 18"), paper scraps, old magazines, brown paper bags, crayons, markers, scissors, glue, pencils.

1. Look at traditional Athabaskan clothing styles.

2. With a pencil, draw an outline of the clothing you wish to make on a brown paper bag. It may be a tunic, trousers, or hood.

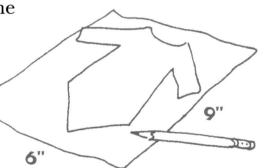

9"

6"

3. Cut out the shape and wrinkle the paper by squeezing it carefully in different directions. This helps give the brown paper bag the look of leather.

4. Smooth out the paper and color with crayon. Use browns, tans, whites, and golds. Put one layer of color over the next. Choose colors you see in leather.

5. Rub a tissue or piece of paper over the layers of crayon. The burnishing smoothes out the colors, mixing them into a glossy leather-like appearance.

6. Cut fringe into strips of paper and glue them onto clothing for decoration.

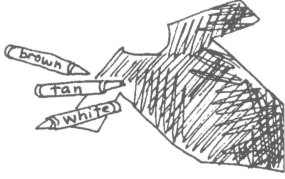

7. Take the 12"x 18" sheet of construction paper and create an environment for your person. Use paper scraps and magazine scraps. Study pictures of interior Alaska.

8. Glue onto this background the clothing you made. Add the arms, legs, feet, head and hands with paper or crayon or marker. You may wish to dress a puppet figure. See instructions on page 24.

9. Color in details.

Caribou and moose tanned leather tunics were sewn and decorated by a hunter's wife. A man's tunic was V-shaped in front, while women often wore a straight hemline. Beads, quillwork, dyed sinew, and shells decorated the yoke of a tunic. An Athabaskan man usually wore earrings and necklaces of shells and beads and had tattoo lines on his chin and cheeks. A neck pouch held an important red "paint stone," obtained in a secret place. The quiver or knife sheath and a beaded pouch containing fire-starting materials would complete his outfit.

Paper Chains

Materials: any large sheet of bright colored paper (butcher paper is preferred, but you may use construction paper, wrapping paper, or newsprint), scissors, pencil, eraser, sponge or rags, tempera paint.

1. Cut the paper into 5" to 7" strips. Choose two or three strips of paper (any color).

2. Fold the strips accordion-style into three or four sections. Cut off any excess paper.

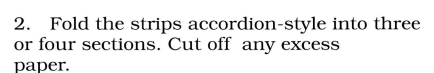

3. With pencil draw a design of a simple arctic animal or object. Make certain that some part of the design extends to the folded sides so that when it is cut out the shapes will be connected.

Hint:
Sponge or rag paint the paper by lightly daubing the cut-out chain. Use markers or crayons too.

4. Cut out the shape. To keep the layers of paper from sliding around while you cut, staple or tape the layers together on the empty part of your design.

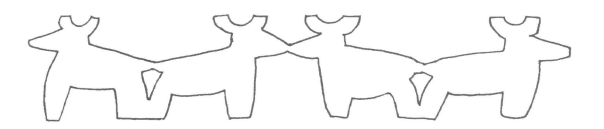

FISH BANNERS

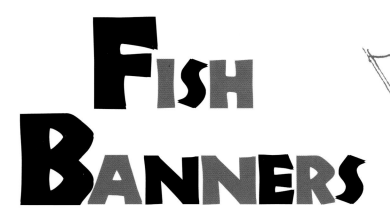

Materials: butcher paper (one piece approximately 24" x 36", any color), markers, watercolors, chalk, cardboard strips, scissors, glue, butcher paper scraps, tissue paper (cut into streamers 1" x 24"), hole punch, string, long sticks, stapler.

1. Fold butcher paper in half matching the long side (36") as shown.

2. Open paper and lay flat on the table. Fold one of the short ends over about two inches. (The cardboard strip will eventually be glued in this fold.)

3. Return paper to its folded position as shown in step 1 but keep the 2" fold on the "inside," as shown.

4. With markers draw a large fish shape on both sides of the paper. The mouth of the fish should be facing the 2" folded edge. Draw the fish using the whole length of the paper.

5. Add details with markers, colored chalk or crayons.

6. Glue on fins, scales, eyes and other features. Let dry. Use watercolors to paint the fish and any empty space. Remember to do both sides. Let dry.

7. Open up the paper and glue the 1"x 24" cardboard strip into the 2" fold. With the help of a friend, staple the cardboard strip into a cylinder form by overlapping the ends slightly. Overlap and glue the 36" sides together.

8. Punch holes in the cardboard, add string and tie or tape to a stick. Add tissue paper streamers on the inside of the tail end.

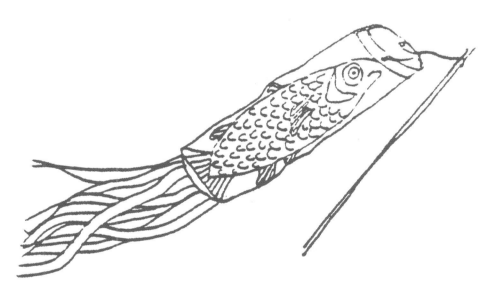

     Fresh, dried, and smoked fish were an important part of the diet of all Alaska Natives. The most important fishing activity for nearly all groups was the seasonal salmon catch. Fishskins were tanned for bags and clothing. The eulochon, or candle fish, were so oily that after they were dried and laced with a wick they were burned like candles. Along the Northwest Coast, halibut were caught with a special bentwood hook. The symbol of the fish appeared on totem poles, crest designs, and in many other Native art forms.

INDEX

ACKNOWLEDGEMENTS

Grateful appreciation to Barbara Baugh,
whose support, encouragement and contributions
made this project a reality.

Appreciation also, to the Anchorage Museum of History and Art for
permission to photograph a portion of its collection. We especially thank
Patrica B. Wolf, Executive Director, Walter Van Horn, Curator of Collections,
Sharon Abbott, Curator of Education and Georgia Blue, Enterprise Director.

The Aleut bentwood hat crafted by Jacob Simeonoff
is used by permission from Koniag, Inc.

Donna Matthews who designed the presentation of the
Northwest Coast design forms on page 8.

A special thanks to:
Denali Elementary School fourth grade students and
their teacher, Mary Doppelfeld.
Terry and Dave Dittman for sharing ideas at each stage.
Jocelyn Young for her professional observations and judgments.
Sharon and Gordon Clawson for their friendship and faith
since the beginning of this project.

Some of the paper crafts were created by Jocelyn Young, Lynn Hallquist,
Lauri Packebush and Molly Bynum.

This project has evolved over the last 10 years with welcomed input from the Alaska Native community. Through these years, there have been changing attitudes, discussions and even legislation affecting Native art. With the general public in mind, decisions have been made regarding the presentation of these materials.

Books for Young Readers

Bartok, Mira. *Alaskan Eskimo and Aleut Stencils.* Glenview, Illinois: Good Year Books, 1994.

Green, Paul, and Abbe Abbott. *I Am Eskimo, Aknik my Name.* Anchorage: Northwest Books, 1959.

Murphy, Claire Rudolf, and Charles Mason. *A Child's Alaska.* Anchorage: Northwest Books, 1994.

Murphy, Claire Rudolf, and Duane Pasco. *The Prince and the Salmon People.* New York: Rizzoli, 1993.

Osinski, Alice. *The Eskimo.* A New True Book: 1992.

Osinski, Alice. *The Tlingit.* A New True Book: 1990.

Younkin, Paula. *Indians of the Arctic and Subarctic: The First Americans Series.* New York: Facts on File, 1992.

Reference Books on Alaska Native Art

Boas, Frank. *Primitive Art.* New York: Dover Publications, 1955.

Fitzhugh, William W., and Susan A. Kaplan. *Inua: Spirit World of the Bering Sea Eskimo.* Washington, D.C.: Smithsonian Institution Press, 1982.

Ray, Dorothy Jean, and Alfred A. Blaker. *Eskimo Masks, Art and Ceremony.* Seattle: University of Washington Press, 1967.

Simeone, William E. *A History of Alaskan Athapaskans.* Anchorage: Anchorage Alaska Historical Commission.

Wardwell, Allen. *Objects of Bright Pride: Northwest Coast Indian Art from the Museum of Natural History.* New York: The Center for InterAmerican Relations, 1978.

NORTHWEST COAST INDIANS

In Alaska, Northwest Coast tribes include — from north to south— the Eyak (ee yak), the Tlingi[t] (klink it), the Tsimhian (shim shee uhn), and the Haida (hi duh). An abundance of food foun[d] at particular locations such as the mouth of the large river allowed these people to inhabit large permanent villages. Over many centuries, they developed an elaborate social structure, a[n] important cycle of ceremonies, and many impressive art forms.

All members of Northwest Coast tribes are born into one of two moieties (moy eh teez), either Eagl[e] (also called Wolf) or Raven, depending on their mother's lineage. Each moiety is further divide[d] into a number of clans, and each clan is also comprised of house groups, which were onc[e] represented by an actual structure which housed many members, both rich and poor. Design[s] which represent specific clans are owned by the clan and cannot be used by others. Permissio[n] must be granted to use or to reproduce them.

Because the climate was mild, Northwest Coast Indians wore twined wool clothing, woven hat[s] of root and bark, and often went barefoot. Both men's and women's arts functioned to make cres[t] designs and to tell clan origin stories and histories. When you see a Northwest Coast object, yo[u] are viewing a story.

The art for which the Northwest Coast Peoples have become most famous is the carving of wood[.] This is a region where totem poles still reach two stories high, where masks are dazzling, an[d] where members of an entire clan may feast from a huge potlatch bowl together.

Objects used in daily life reflect their distinctive art style. "Northwest Coast Style" is character[-] ized by a firm, black line outlining eyes, joints, ears, ribs, teeth, mouths, and other features o[f] the animals and birds. The artists' creativity was expressed by the way in which the spaces wer[e] filled.

NORTHWEST COAST INDIAN PHOTOGRAPH - PAGE 4-5
Can you find these items in the picture?

1. Chilkat woven apron with puffin beaks, deer hooves and trade cloth
2. Halibut hook
3. Northwest Coast carved rifle
4. Frontlet mask depicting beaver with ermine, abalone shells and sea lion whiskers
5. Small hawk mask
6. Octopus carved dish with trade beads
7. Hawk design salmon club
8. Speaker staff
9. Carved wooden bentwood box

The potlatch (a Chinook term which means "to give") was a commemorative celebration accompanied by much feasting and dancing, climaxe[d] by the giving of elaborate gifts. A potlatch was held when a house was built or named or when a certain period had elapsed after an importan[t] person's death. Masks, coppers, and other status symbols such as articles of clothing, dishes and utensils were made to be given away a[t] the event which might last several days. The inventory of goods often filled an entire room. While a potlatch may bring a challenge for th[e] guest to outdo the host in the future, it was also a way of keeping resources balanced within the community.

THE ALEUTS

When contact was made with Aleutian peoples during the mid 1700's by Russian hunters i[n] search of furs, the results were brutal and devastating. The maritime skills of Aleut men wer[e] exploited by the Russians, who took many men from their homes to search for sea otters. Afte[r] less than one hundred years of such labor and accompanying illnesses brought by the invaders[,] the Aleut population had been decimated and the fur-bearing animals were nearly extinct. Ove[r] time Aleut and Russian people blended a productive culture as we know it today.

The art forms of the Aleuts, even during the long period of Russian domination, remained vibran[t] and strong. Finely twined grass mats were woven by women to cloak mummies—beloved famil[y] members and legendary hunters—after their burial. Twining was also used to produc[e] containers which evolved into the finest grass baskets ever developed, usually known as "Att[u] baskets." Aleut women also sewed a variety of fine garments including birdskin cloaks and coat[s] as well as long *kamleikas* made of intestine. Aleut men steamed, bent and decorated ornat[e] wooden hats and visors which they wore when hunting on the open sea to assume a birdlik[e] appearance.

ALEUT PHOTOGRAPH - PAGE 28-29
Can you find these items in the picture?

1. Puffin beak ceremonial rattle
2. Sea mammal intestine wall pouch
3. Sea otter harpoon with copper point
4. Small grass woven basket
5. Medium grass woven basket
6. Large grass woven basket
7. Wooden throwing board
8. Medium basket lid

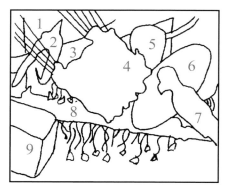

NORTHWEST COAST

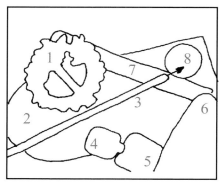

ALEUT

THE YUPIK, INUPIAT, ALUTIIQ, AND ST. LAWRENCE ISLAND ESKIMOS OF ALASKA

The spiritual world of all Eskimo peoples, in particular the Yupik, was very rich. Nearly all things, whether a rock, a human, or a caribou, had a soul, one type of which was an *inua*. All Eskimos believed that a group of spirits controlled their relationship with the natural world, providing an abundance of game, and that these spirits must be celebrated and respected. An *inua* in the form of a small human face can often be seen carved into the center of a mask or peering out of some portion of a carving. This human-like image underscores the dependence between men and animals, a key part of these belief systems.

In pre-contact Eskimo society, nothing was wasted. Native peoples were the original recyclers, and what could not be used was returned to the earth, as evidenced by archeological research today. Private property was not an important concept among Eskimo peoples, but their possessions were almost always finely crafted and rich in decoration. Such objects demonstrated the wealth of the family, the skill of the maker, and the prowess of the family hunter. Jewelry and hair ornaments made of trade beads and ivory were worn by women, who also tattooed their faces with symbolic designs, and made and decorated their clothing with skill. Most of the traditional art forms practiced by both men and women are still being done, and taught, today. These include skin sewing, wood carving, bone and ivory etching, and mask making. The performing arts —storytelling, ceremonial dancing and drumming—saw a decline through missionary influence during this century, but are now being revitalized throughout all Eskimo homelands.

ESKIMO PHOTOGRAPH - PAGE 38-39
Can you find these items in the picture?

1. Eskimo gut parka with feather and bird beak trim from St. Lawrence Island
2. Engraved musk ox horn used to pound blubber by Canadian Eskimos
3. Inupiat pieced cap with bird beak and feathers
4. Dance headband with caribou fur
5. Inupiat caribou teeth belt
6. Housekeeping bag
7. Carved walrus ivory cribbage board
8. Goose body bag
9. St. Lawrence Island leather ball with beads and yarn trim
10. Mukluks of seal fur and land mammal fur
11. Wooden carved bowl with painted figure
12. Fish skin mittens
13. Feather

THE ATHABASKANS

The Athabaskans followed the seasonal migrations of fish and game, which restricted them to portable belongings. Their garments were simply but efficiently constructed of moose and caribou hide, often decorated with fine geometric porcupine quillwork or painted red ochre designs. The wealth they had, they wore. An Athabaskan chief a century ago might have had more than 1,000 dentalium shells sewn on his tunic, a symbol not only of his prosperity, but of his success in trading with other groups.

The Athabaskans are renowned for their birch bark industry. Today, women and girls stitch traditional bead designs onto hand-crafted leather mittens, slippers, pouches and wall decorations.

ATHABASKAN PHOTOGRAPH - PAGE 62-63
Can you find these items in the picture?

1. Babiche woven hunting bag
2. Birch bark basket
3. Birch bark basket
4. Blue woolen shirt with red trim and dentalium shells
5. Beaded mittens of moose hide and fur with braided yarn tie
6. Birch bark basket
7. Puffin beak ceremonial rattles
8. Birch bark basket
9. Feathered ceremonial head piece

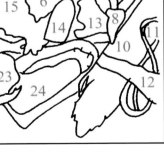

PAGES INSIDE COVER

1. Leather
2. Whale bone
3. Abalone
4. Fox fur
5. Sinew
6. Babiche bag
7. Coiled bark
8. Halibut hook
9. Stone dish
10. Dried grass
11. Braided wool yarn
12. Horn ladle
13. Antler
14. Bone
15. Feathers
16. Copper knife with ivory handle
17. Trade beads
18. Sea mammal intestine
19. Birch bark basket
20. Baleen
21. Musk ox horn
22. Ermine fur
23. Rabbit fur
24. Fish skin mittens
25. Baleen wolf hunter

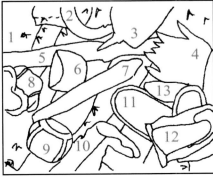

ESKIMO

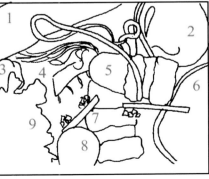

ATHABASKAN

Hands-on Alaska
(ISBN 0-9643177-3-7)

Books from
KITS PUBLISHING

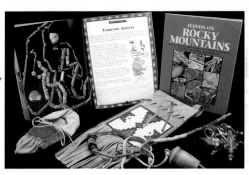

Hands-on Rocky Mountains
(ISBN 0-9643177-2-9)

Consider these books for:
the library
teaching social studies
art
multicultural programs
ESL programs
museum programs
community youth events
home schooling

Hands-on Latin America
(ISBN 0-9643177-1-0)

Hands-on Celebrations
(ISBN 0-9643177-4-5)

Hands-on Pioneers
(ISBN 1-57345-085-5)

Hands-on Africa
(ISBN 0-9643177-7-X)

Hands-on Asia
(ISBN 0-9643177-5-3)

KITS ON ALASKA AND CANADIAN NATIVE CULTURES

Yvonne Merrill developed portable, interactive and interdisciplinary kits as a result of her twelve years of work with the Anchorage History and Art Museum and as an Art Specialist with the Anchorage School District. They are the foundation for the *Hands-on Alaska* book. These kits are now available to programs that value quality replication of authentic artifacts and interactive study:

THE NATIVE ART KIT

The kits are designed to be displayed as cultural centers. Art projects are clearly presented. An illustrated manual enhances and informs the instructor about the rich and varied topic of the art of Eskimos, Athabaskans, Northwest Coast Indians and Aleuts.

THE EARLY CHILD TEACHING KIT
PRESCHOOL TO 2ND GRADE

This unique tool invites young people to explore map sites, wear objects, study myths, use puppets, and appreciate many important traditions.

NORTHWEST COAST INDIAN KIT

The art, myths, architecture, and culture of the people in this region is presented with original drawings, fine color prints and hands-on replicated objects.

THE ATHABASKANS CULTURAL KIT

The story of the Athabaskan nomadic culture emphasizes bark projects, tools, geography and contemporary arts.

THE ESKIMO CULTURAL KIT

The cultures of the Bering Coast Yupik people and the Inupiat Eskimos have similarities and differences. The resources and their use translates into a cultural story of traditional art.

The kits range in price from $500 to $2,000. An Inservice is essential. Kit production involves a six-month advance order and deposit. The kits are copyrighted, have original illustrations, many hand-crafted items and are designed for classroom use, museums and community enrichment services. For more information, call 801-582-2517.